GARDEN PRAYERS: SUMMER

T.M. Givens

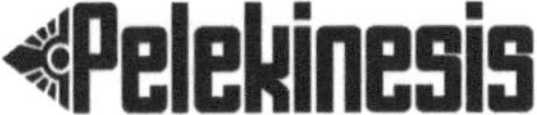

Pelekinesis

Garden Prayers: Summer by T.M. Givens

ISBN: 978-1-949790-21-4

Layout and book design by Mark Givens
Artwork by T.M. Givens

First Pelekinesis Printing 2020

For information:

Pelekinesis, 112 Harvard Ave #65, Claremont, CA 91711 USA

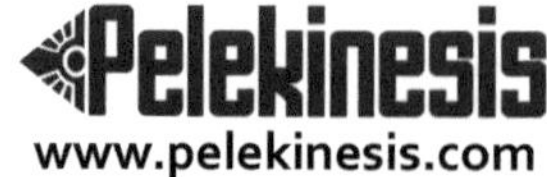

GARDEN PRAYERS: SUMMER

T.M. Givens

Still dedicated to my one and only Carolyne,
without whom I wouldn't see clearly.
and
Rainier Maria Rilke
Robert Crumb
Diane Arbus

I think I'm beginning to understand this whole drawing business. Sometimes it comes easily ..... I just start and finish in one day, and without much thought ..... and then, sometimes it's a real struggle ..... starts out good and then goes haywire ..... I'm not sure what is the difference ..... I know all the advice is helpful and well-meaning, but words sometimes don't help me much ..... what are those dark things ..... how are they dark and then become light ..... science tells me reasons, but I'm not sure that's all ..... I can tell you how beautiful I think that is ..... but can I tell you why or show you why ....

The drawings in this book are still based on the idea that they are prayers ..... what about if I don't have enough good words to let you know what I believe or that I'm thinking ..... can you understand that well enough?

It's hard to communicate without words ..... we learn so much about this and still sometimes don't communicate well enough ..... is there some other way I need to learn ....

Today, it's raining and as I look out my window, the trees just got trimmed and I can see the differences between the strength of the limbs and the beginning of growths ..... and the way the wind blows the rose bush in front of the trees ..... and the cars moving quickly by and the stillness of the great canyon just beyond the road ..... it's fenced in, but I can still see beyond the fence because I'm up a little higher.

Terry
Sometime in 2020

Each drawing is made while on-site with a Faber Castell (SX) India ink pen on Strathmore Bristol Smooth Surface drawing paper and then finished in my studio with Prismacolor pencils, both Premier and Thinline models.

First Summer Prayer

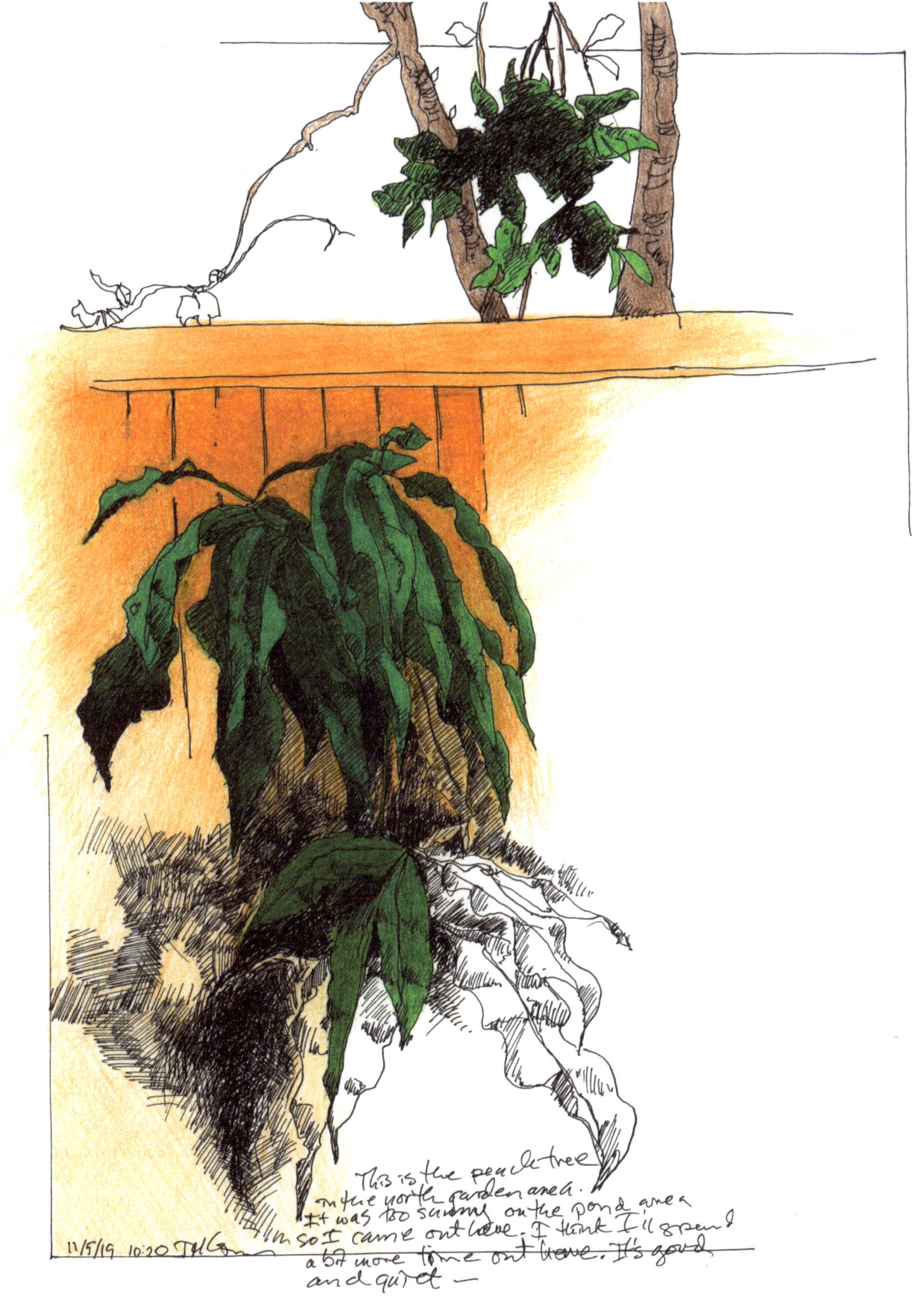
This is the peach tree
in the north garden area.
It was too sunny on the pond area
so I came out here. I think I'll spend
a bit more time out here. It's good
and quiet —
11/5/19 10:20 TH Car

Second Summer Prayer

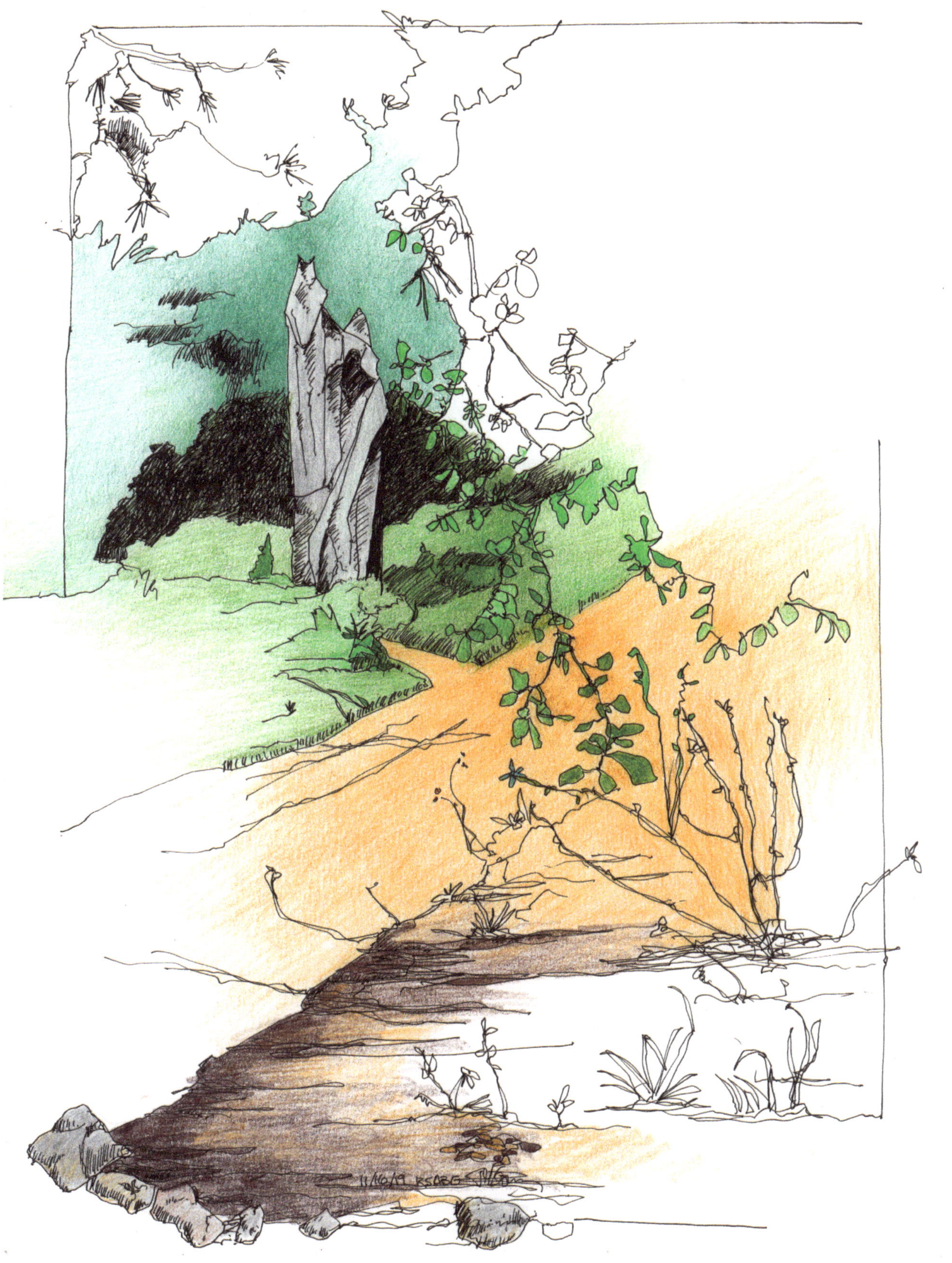
11/16/19 ksaeg

Third Summer Prayer

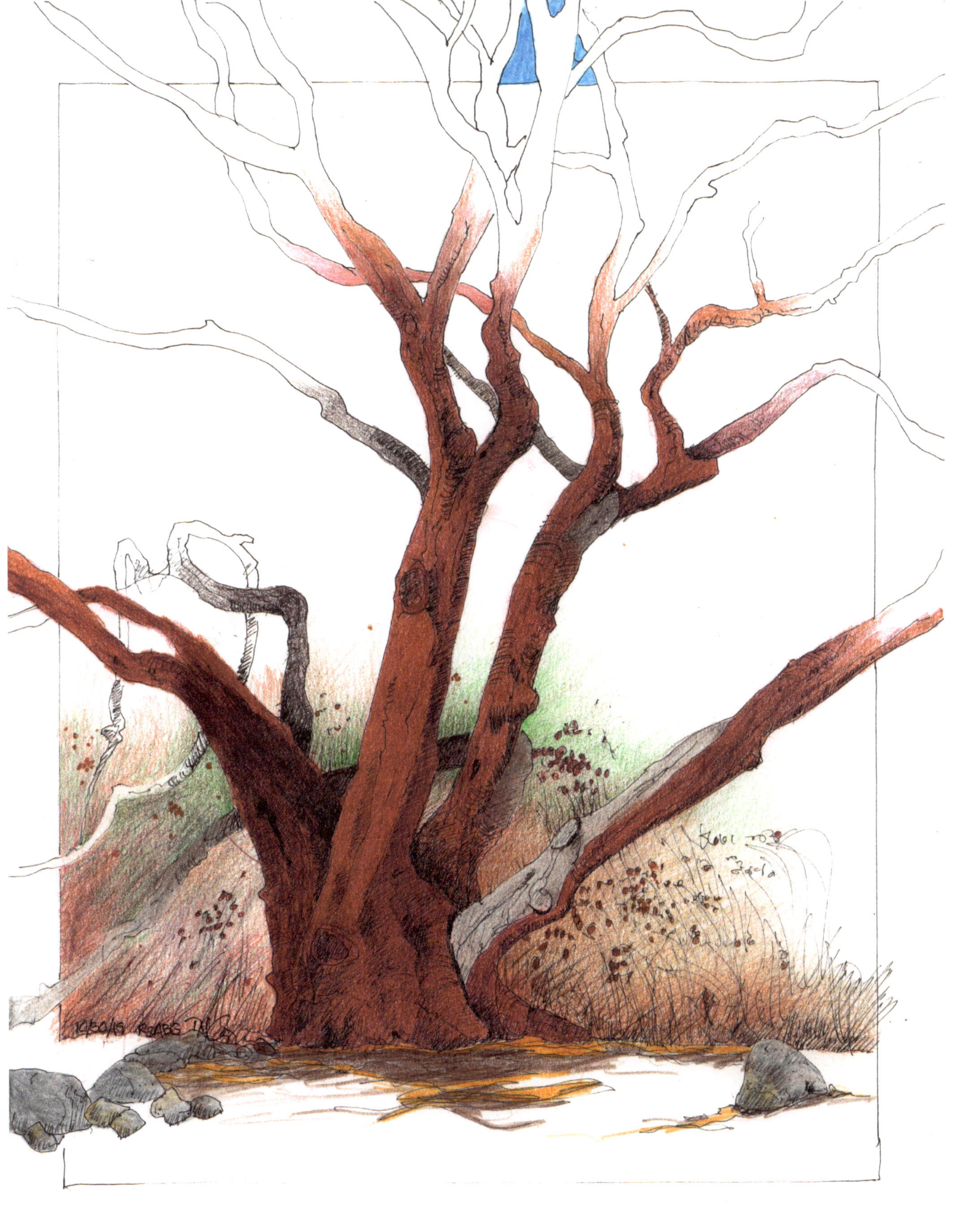

Fourth Summer Prayer

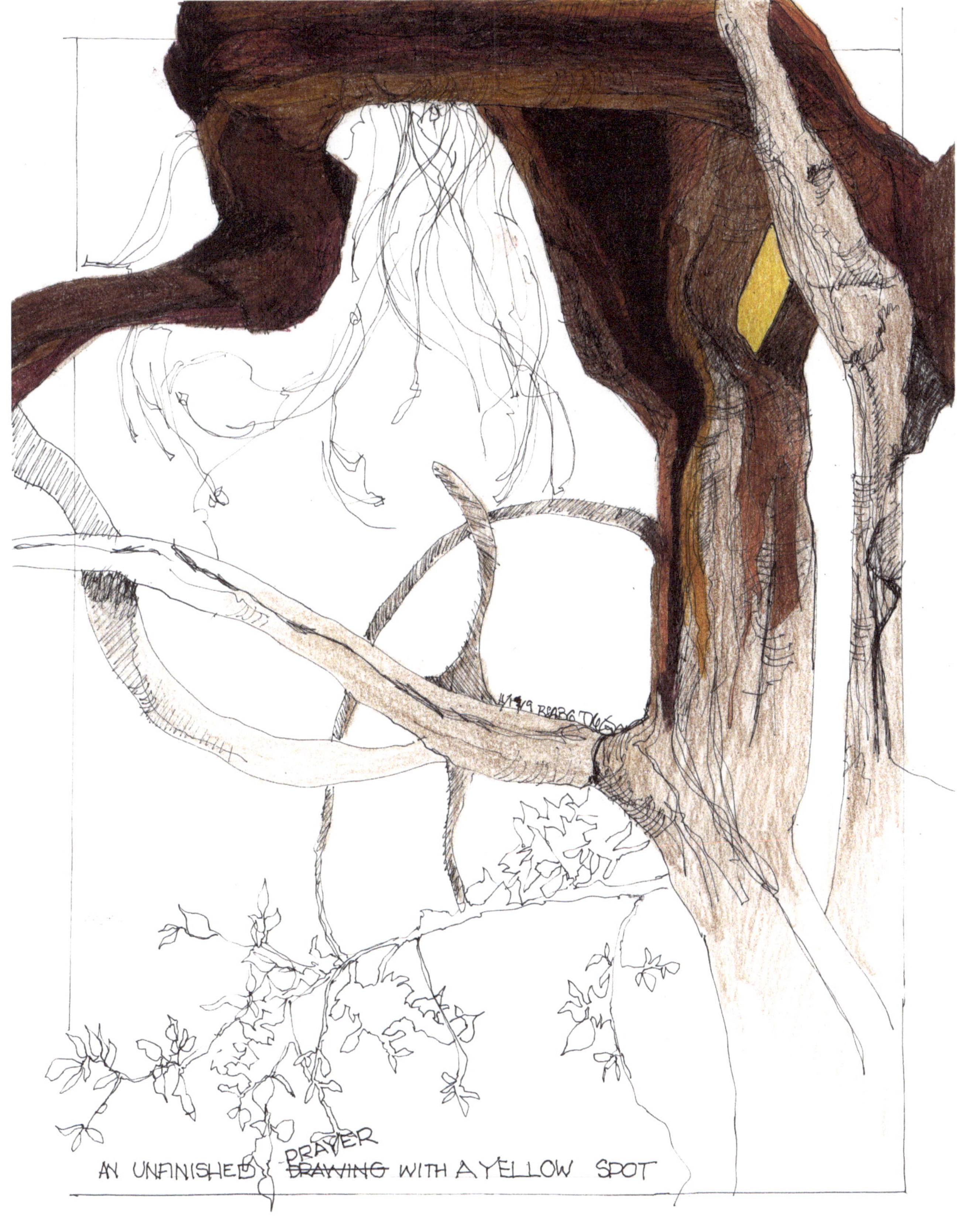

AN UNFINISHED PRAYER ~~DRAWING~~ WITH A YELLOW SPOT

Fifth Summer Prayer

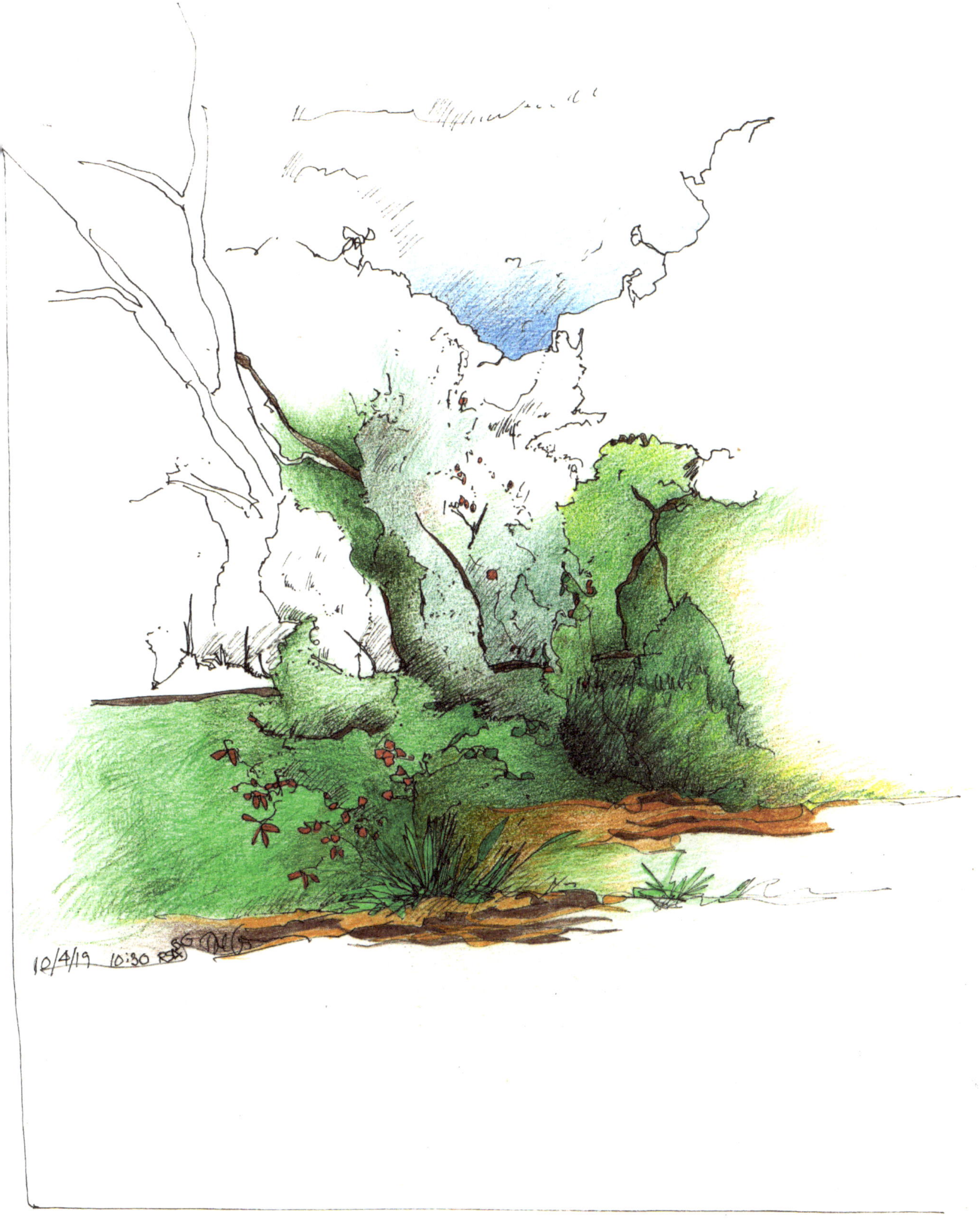

10/4/19 10:30 RBG

Sixth Summer Prayer

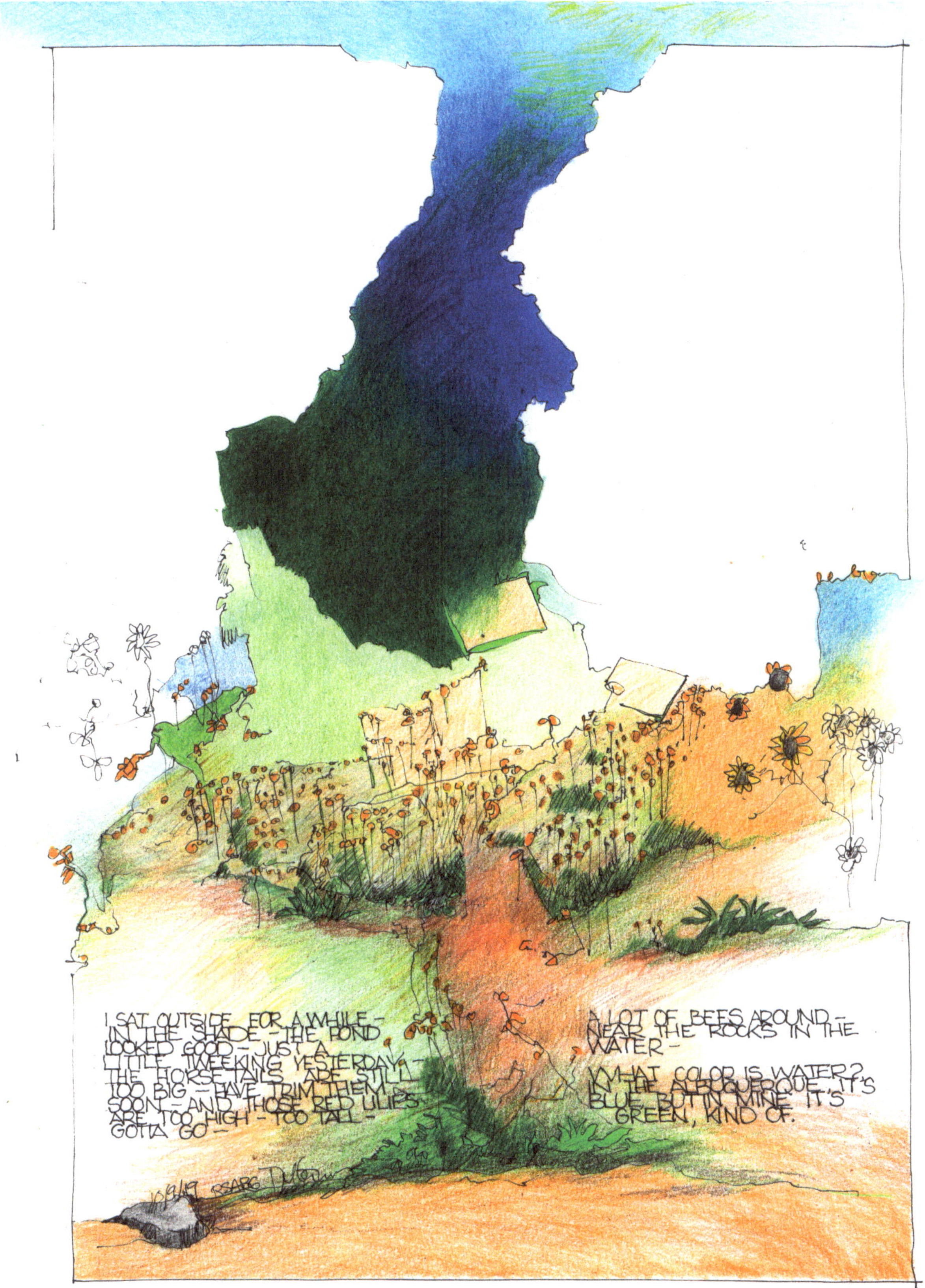

I SAT OUTSIDE FOR A WHILE –
IN THE SHADE – THE POND
LOOKED GOOD – JUST A
LITTLE TWEEKING YESTERDAY –
THE HORSETAILS ARE STILL
TOO BIG – HAVE TRIM THEM
SOON – AND THOSE RED LILIES
ARE TOO HIGH – TOO TALL –
GOTTA GO –

A LOT OF BEES AROUND –
NEAR THE ROCKS IN THE
WATER –

WHAT COLOR IS WATER?
IN THE ALBUQUERQUE, IT'S
BLUE BUT IN MINE IT'S
GREEN, KIND OF.

Seventh Summer Prayer

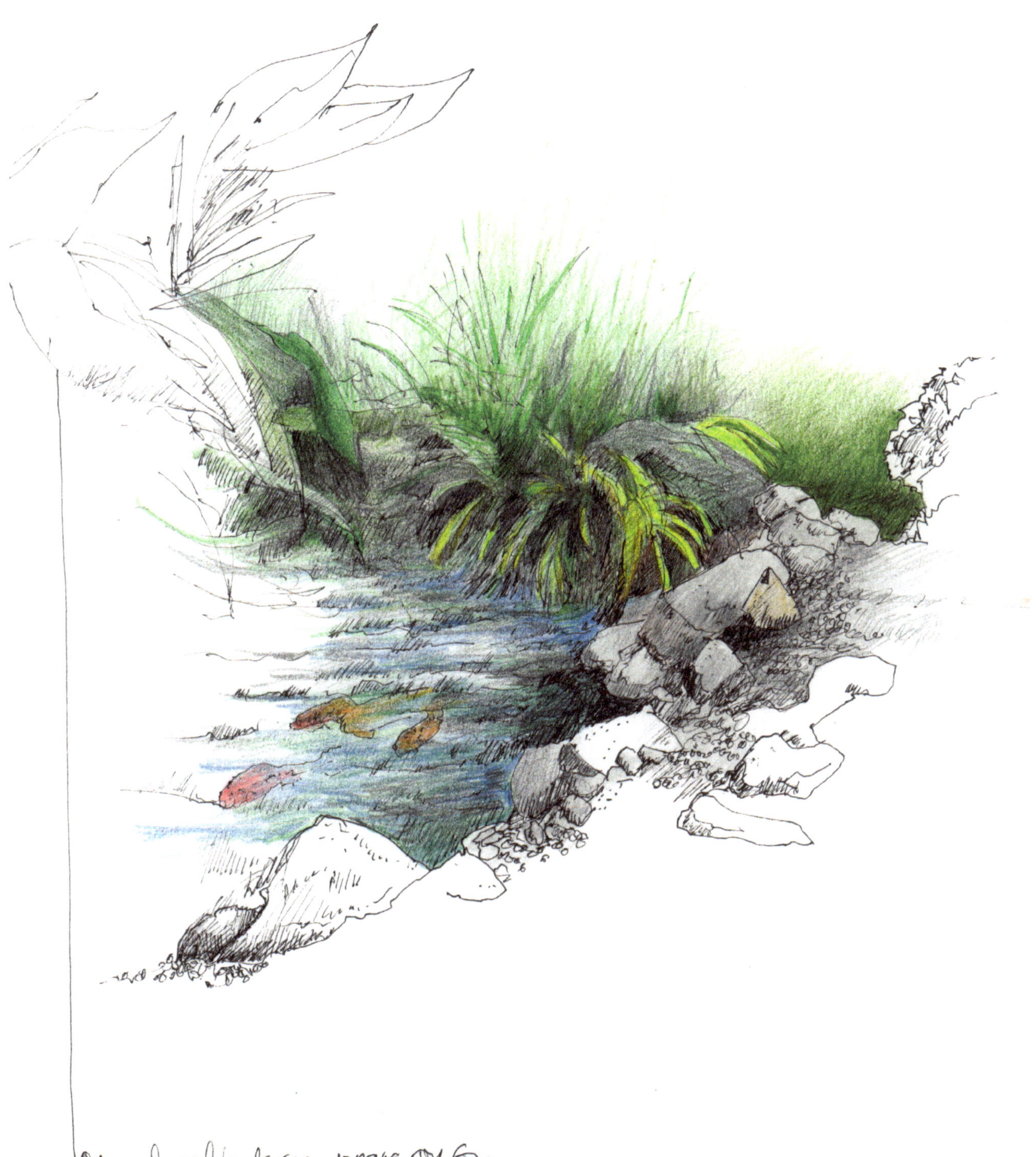

Our pond and landscape with Koi 10/29/19 TM.G

Eighth Summer Prayer

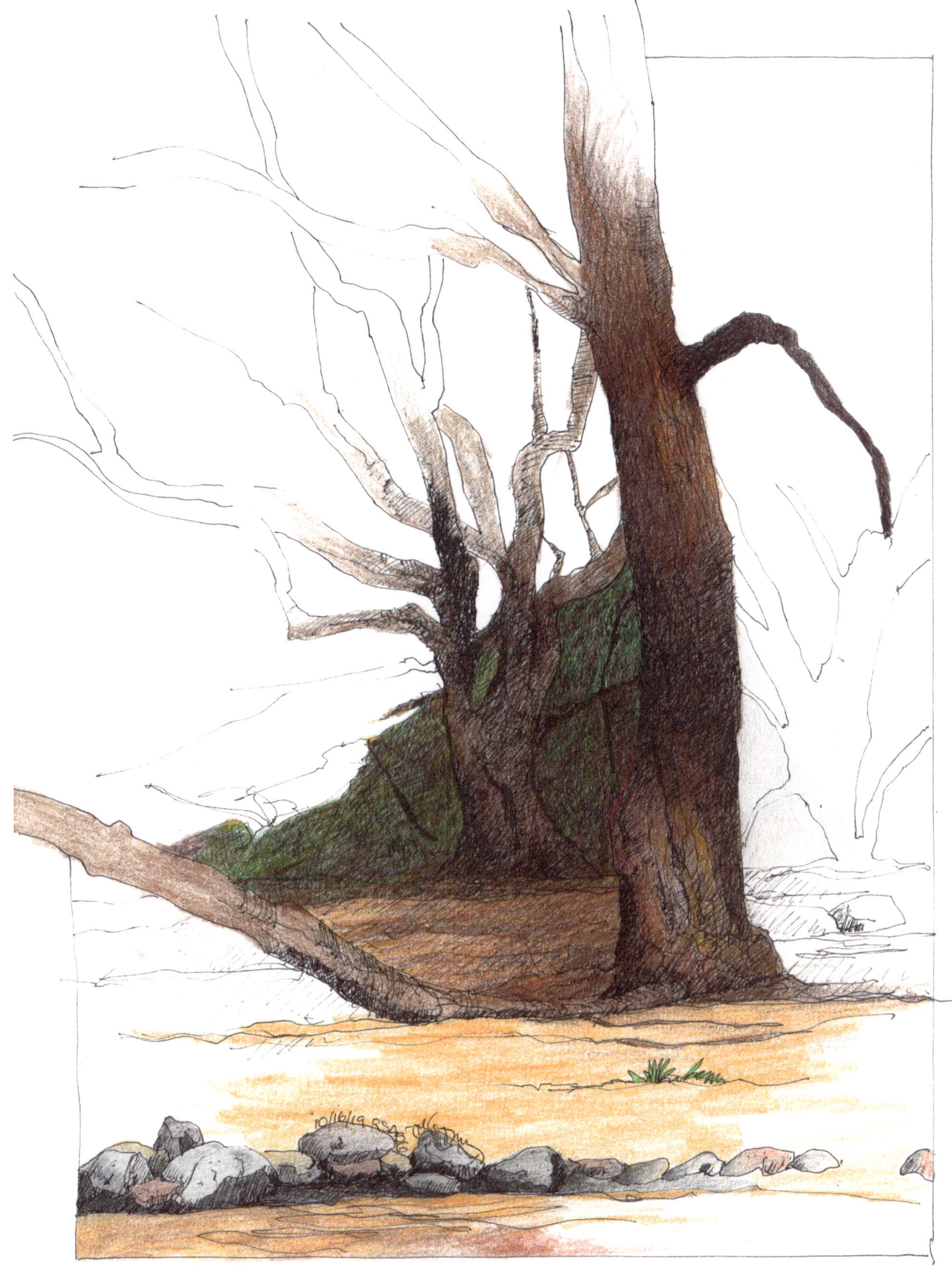

10/16/19 RSA

Ninth Summer Prayer

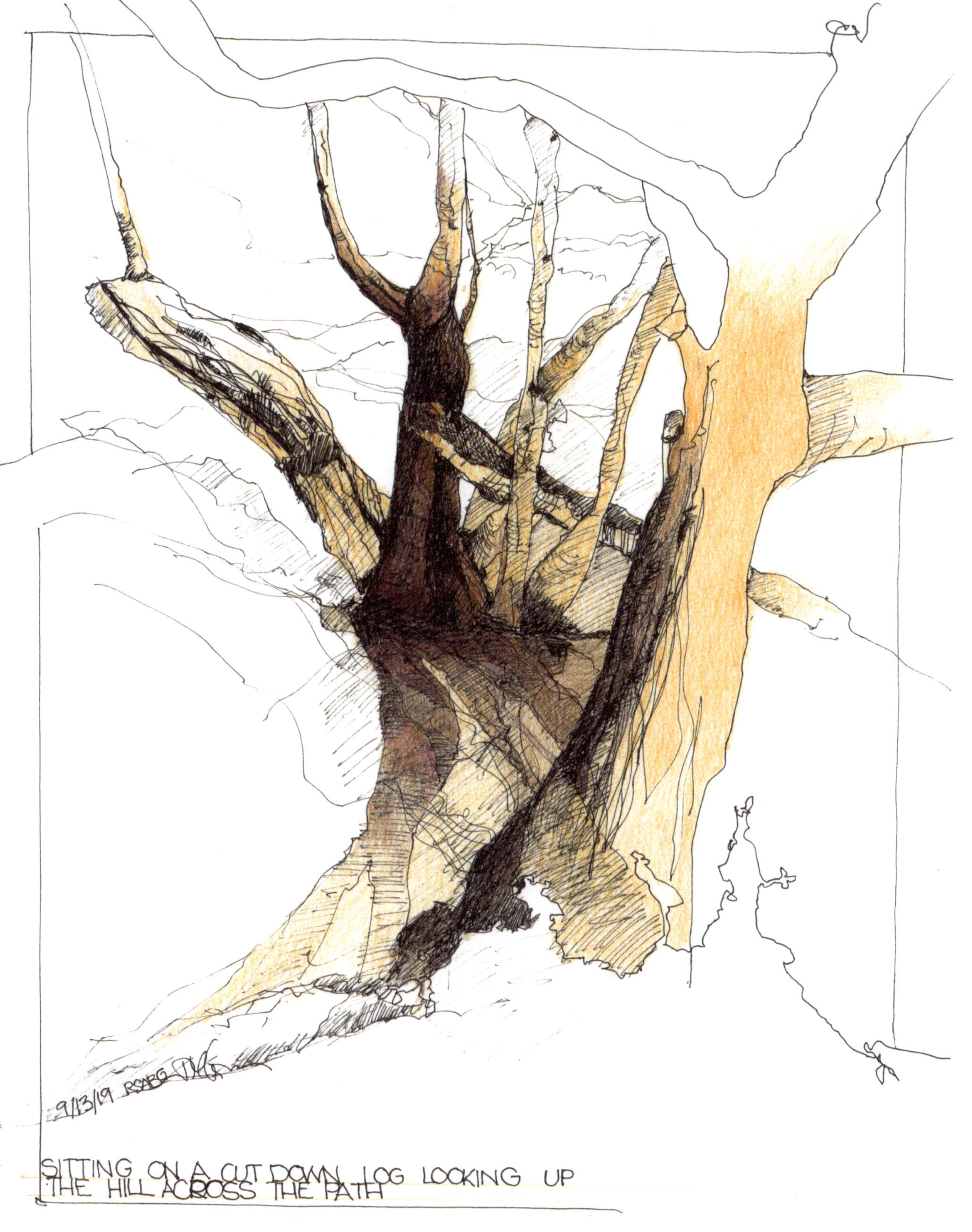

9/13/19
SITTING ON A CUT DOWN LOG LOOKING UP
THE HILL ACROSS THE PATH

Tenth Summer Prayer

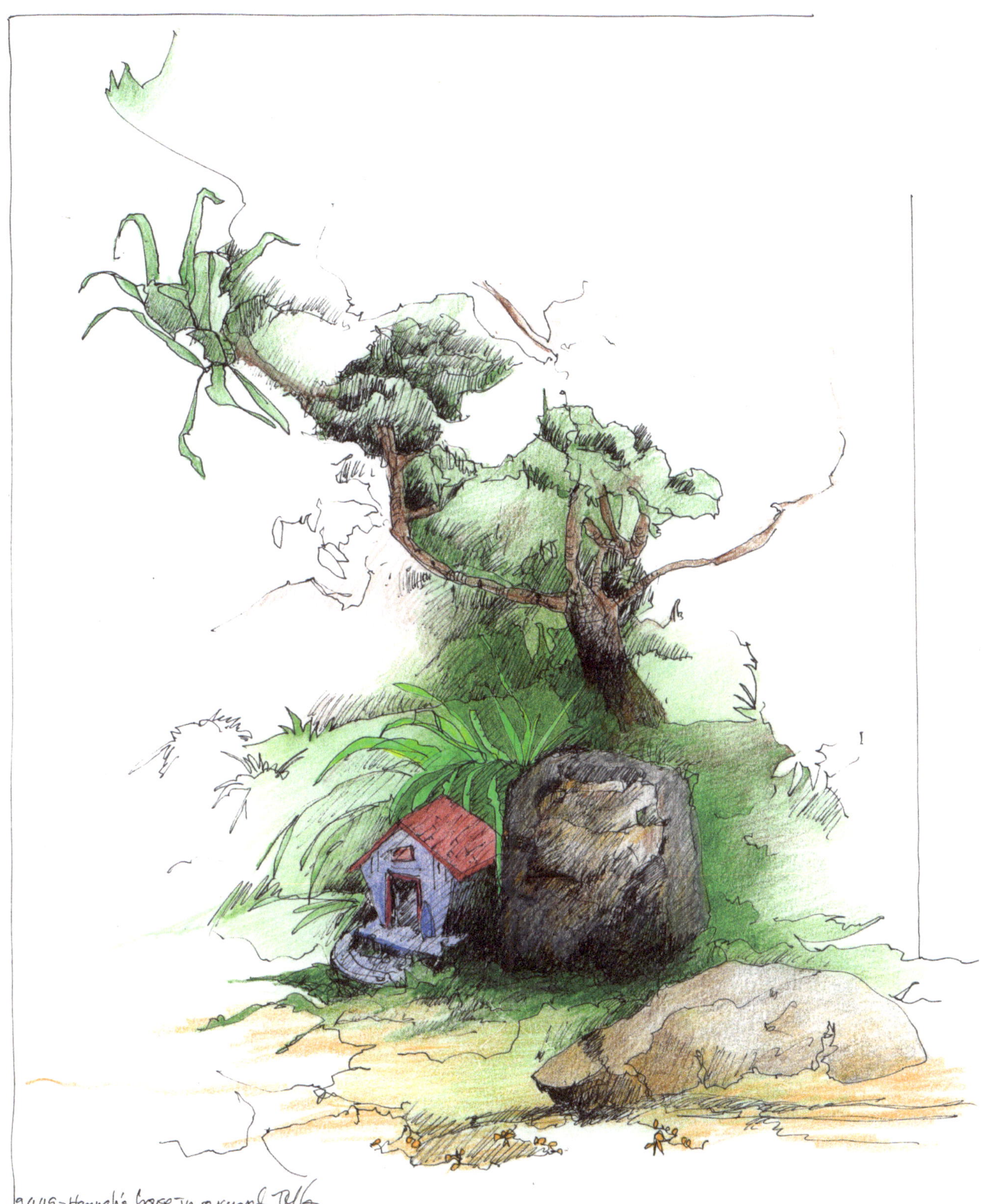

9/1/19 – Hannah's house in our yard

Eleventh Summer Prayer

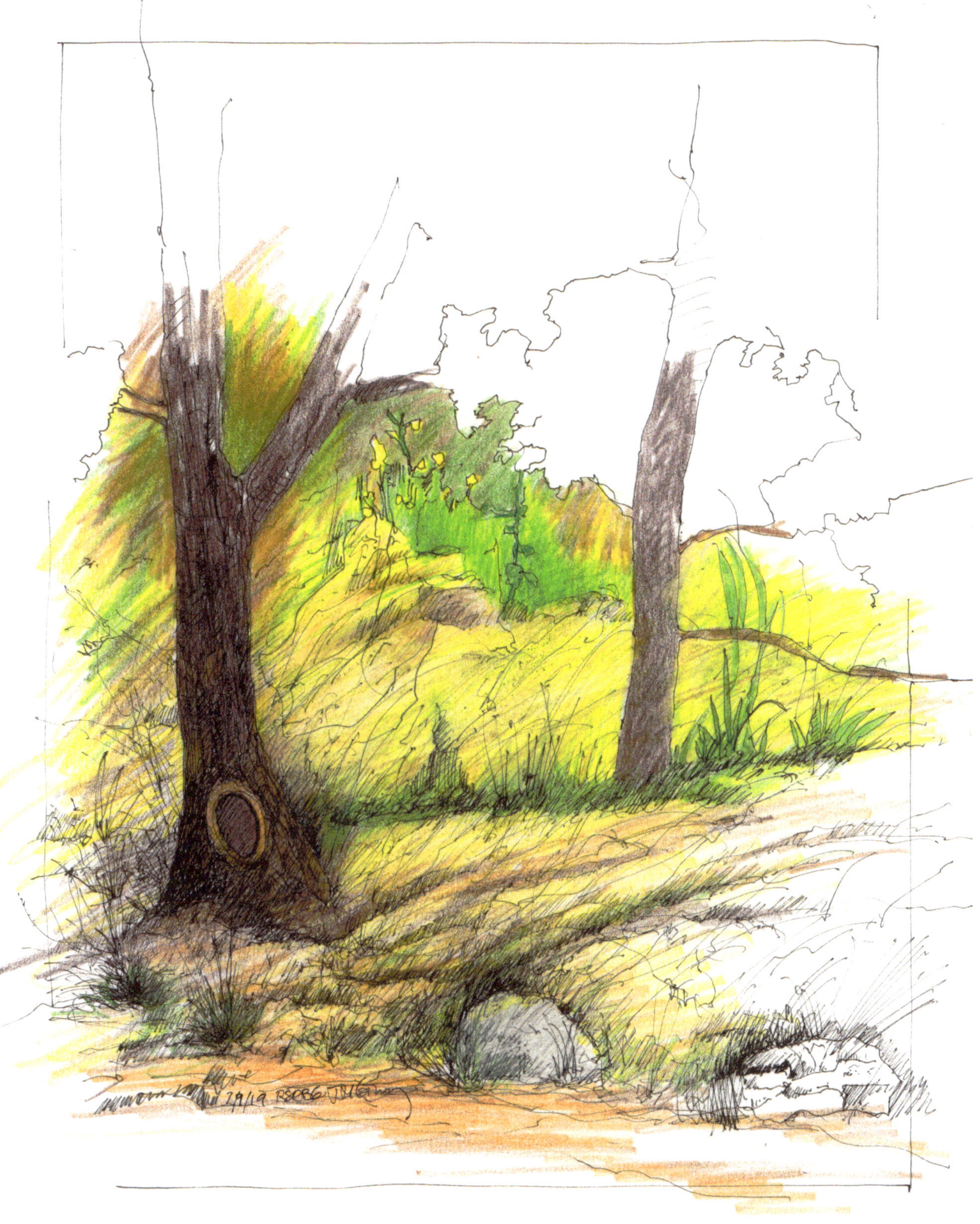

Twelfth Summer Prayer

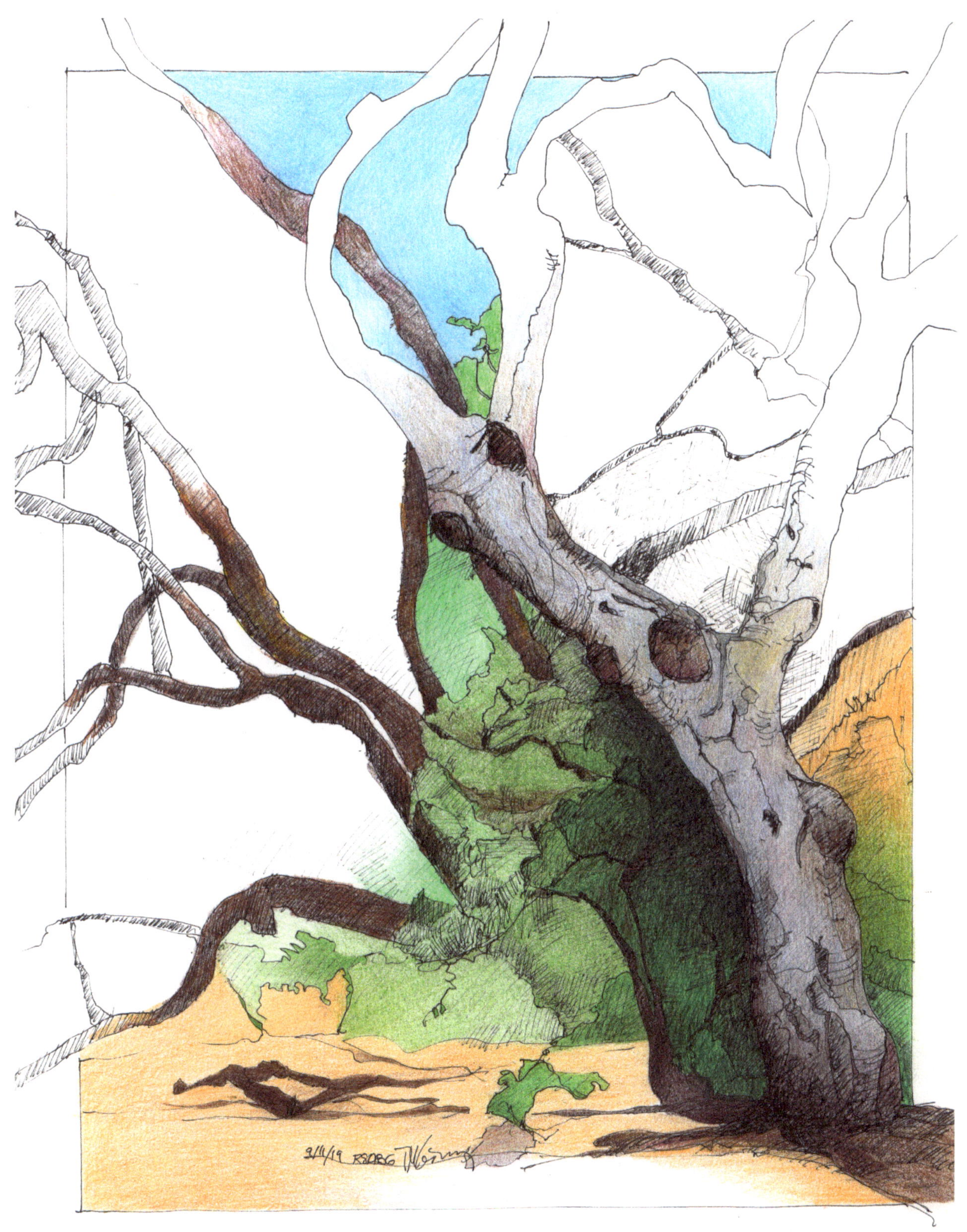

Thirteenth Summer Prayer

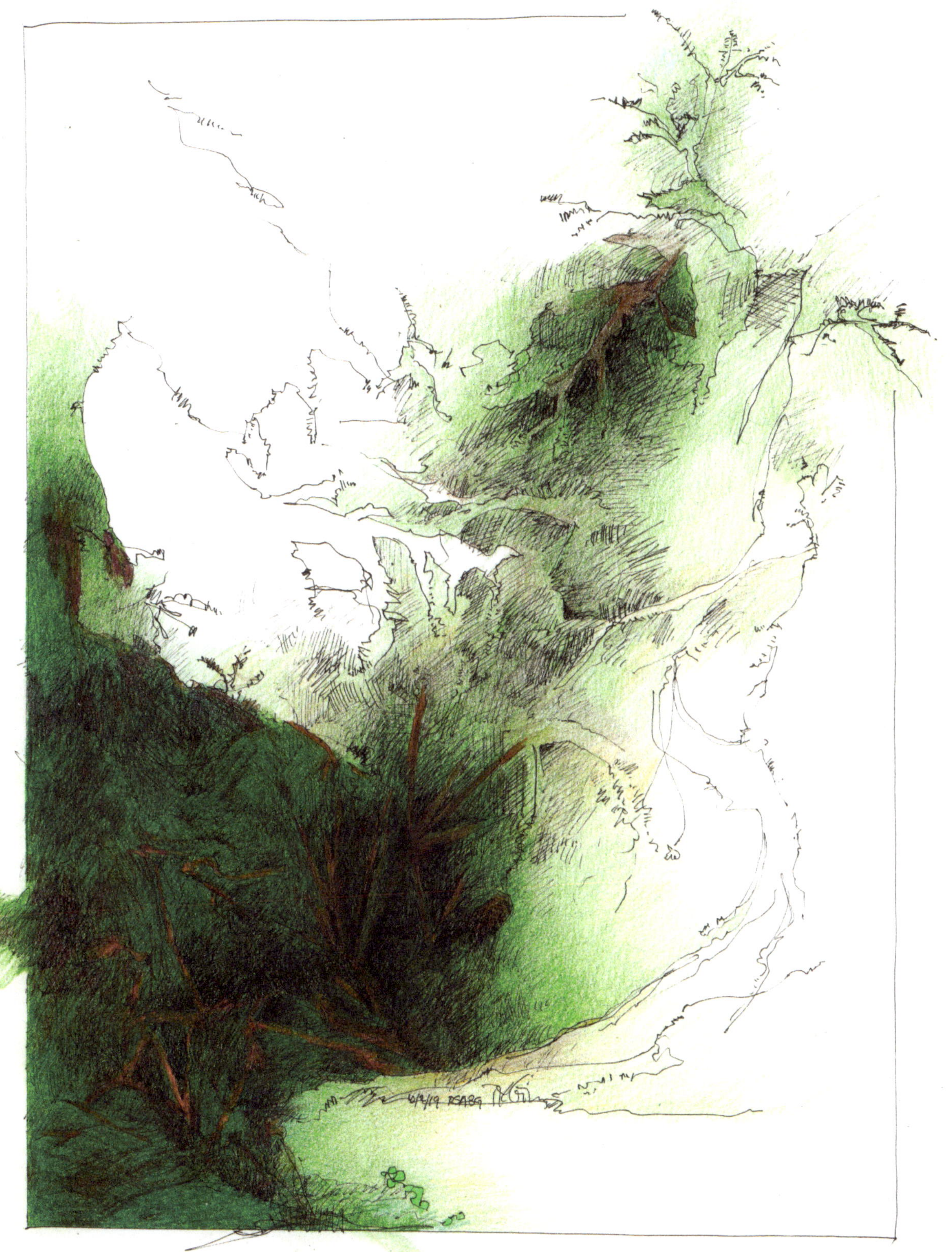
6/4/19 RSABG

Fourteenth Summer Prayer

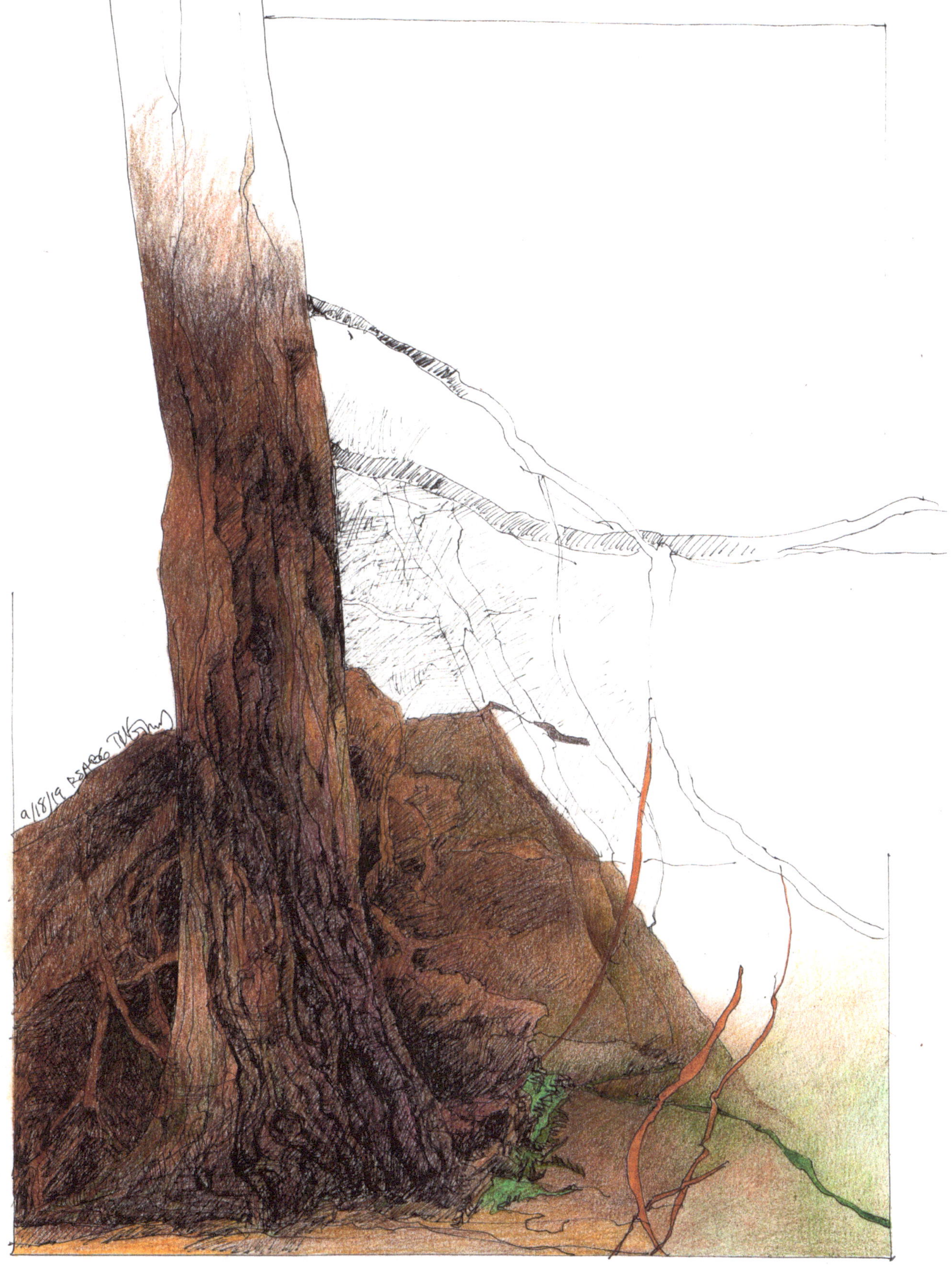
9/18/19

Fifteenth Summer Prayer

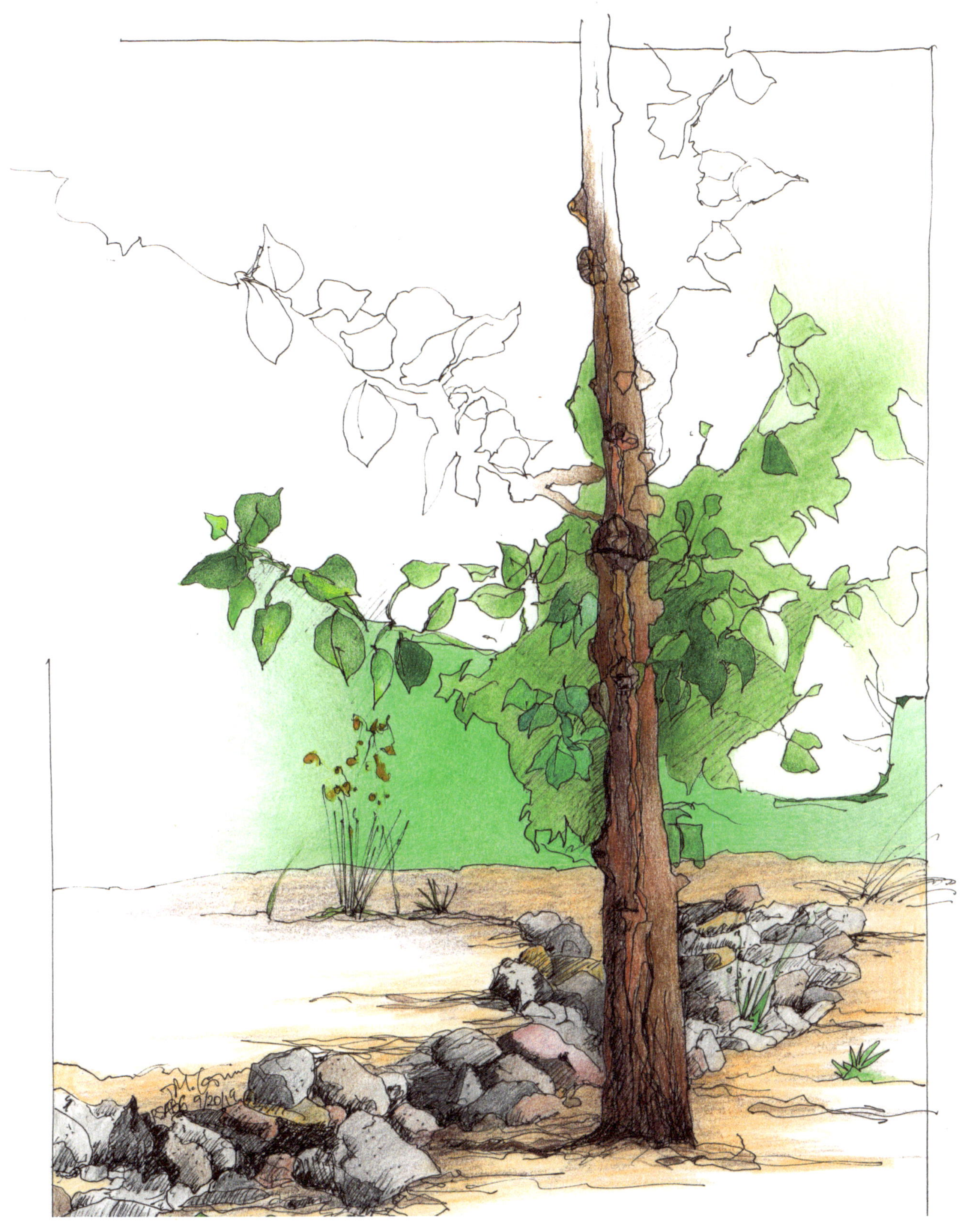

Sixteenth Summer Prayer

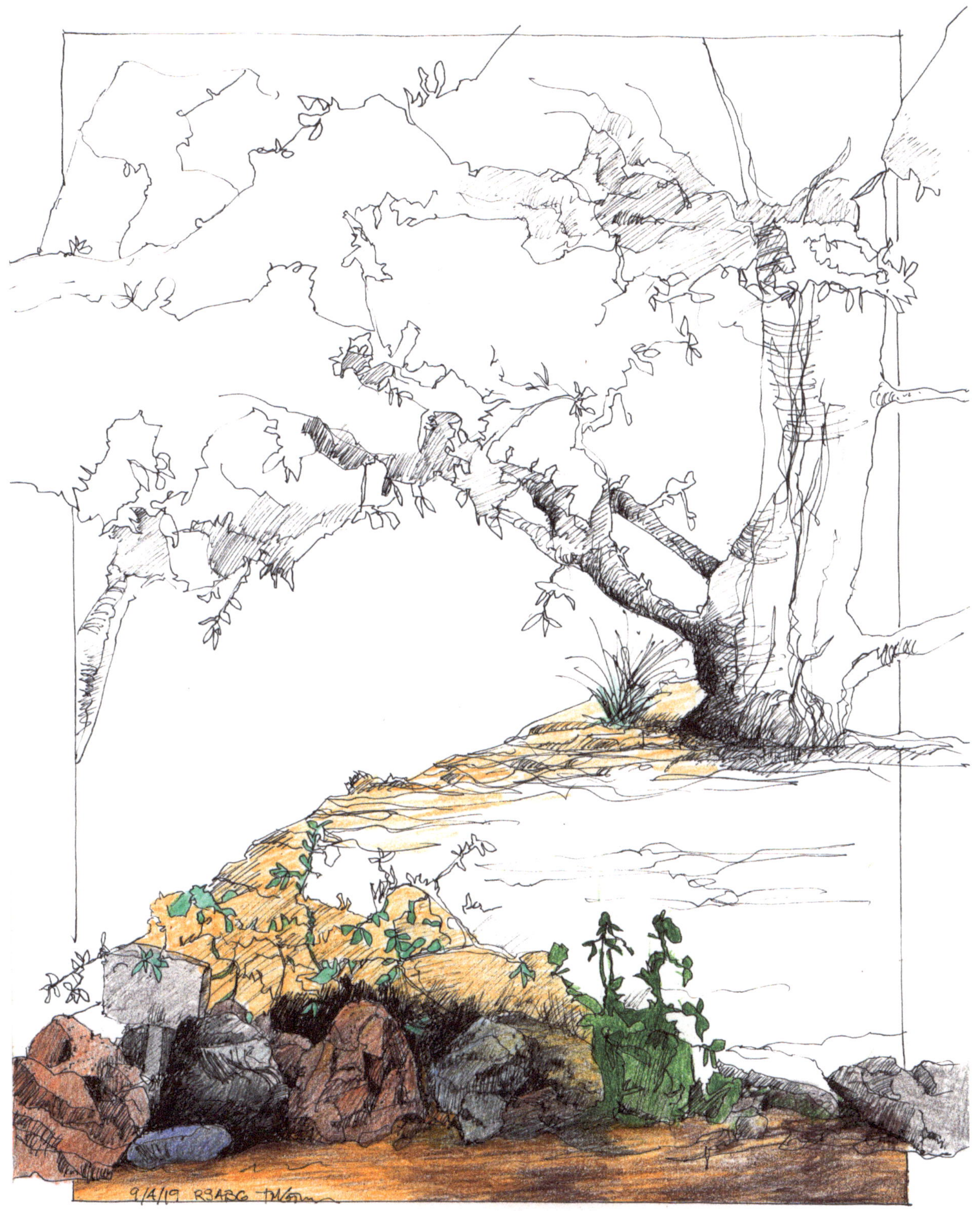
9/4/19 RGABG TW/cm

Seventeenth Summer Prayer

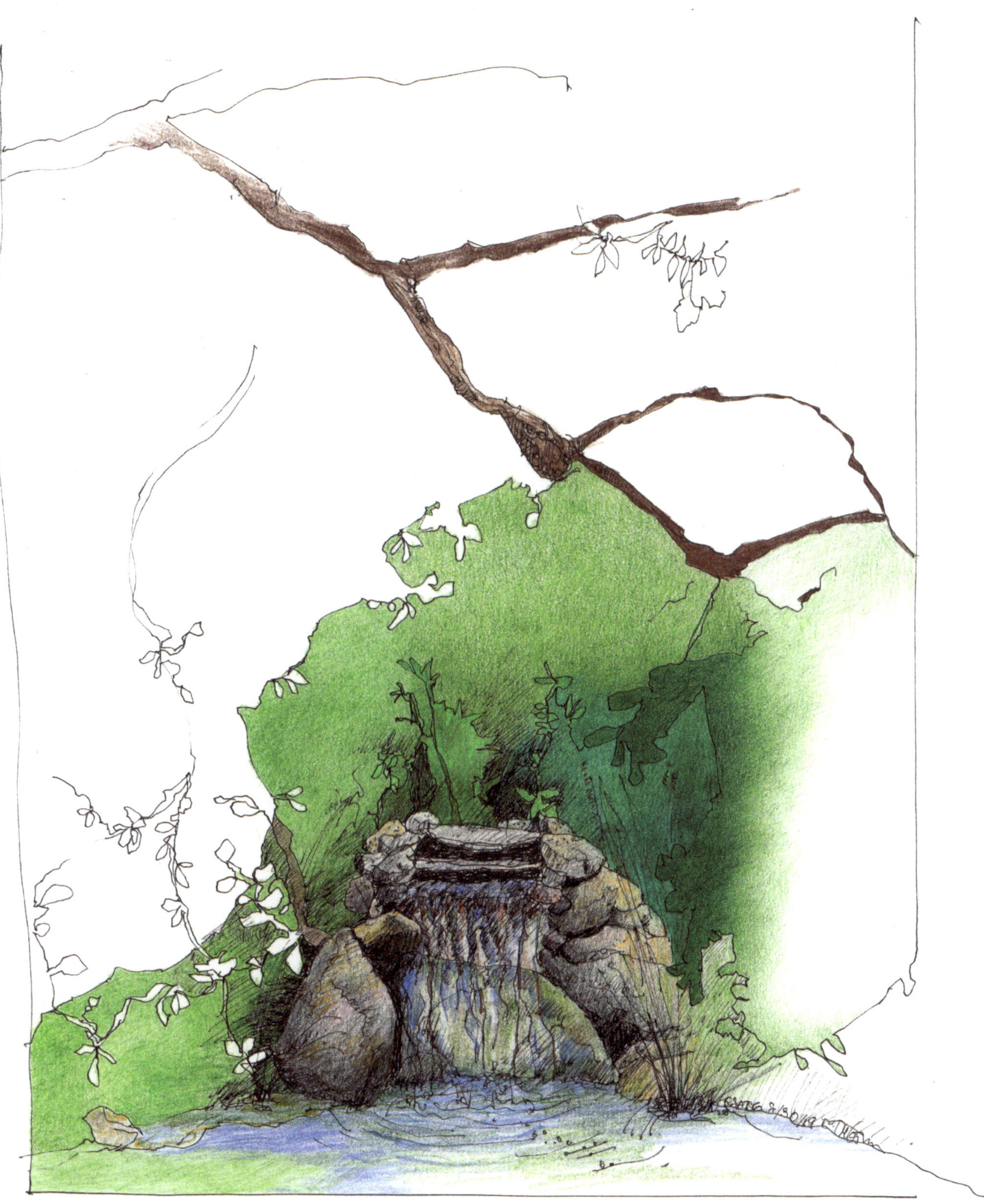

Eighteenth Summer Prayer

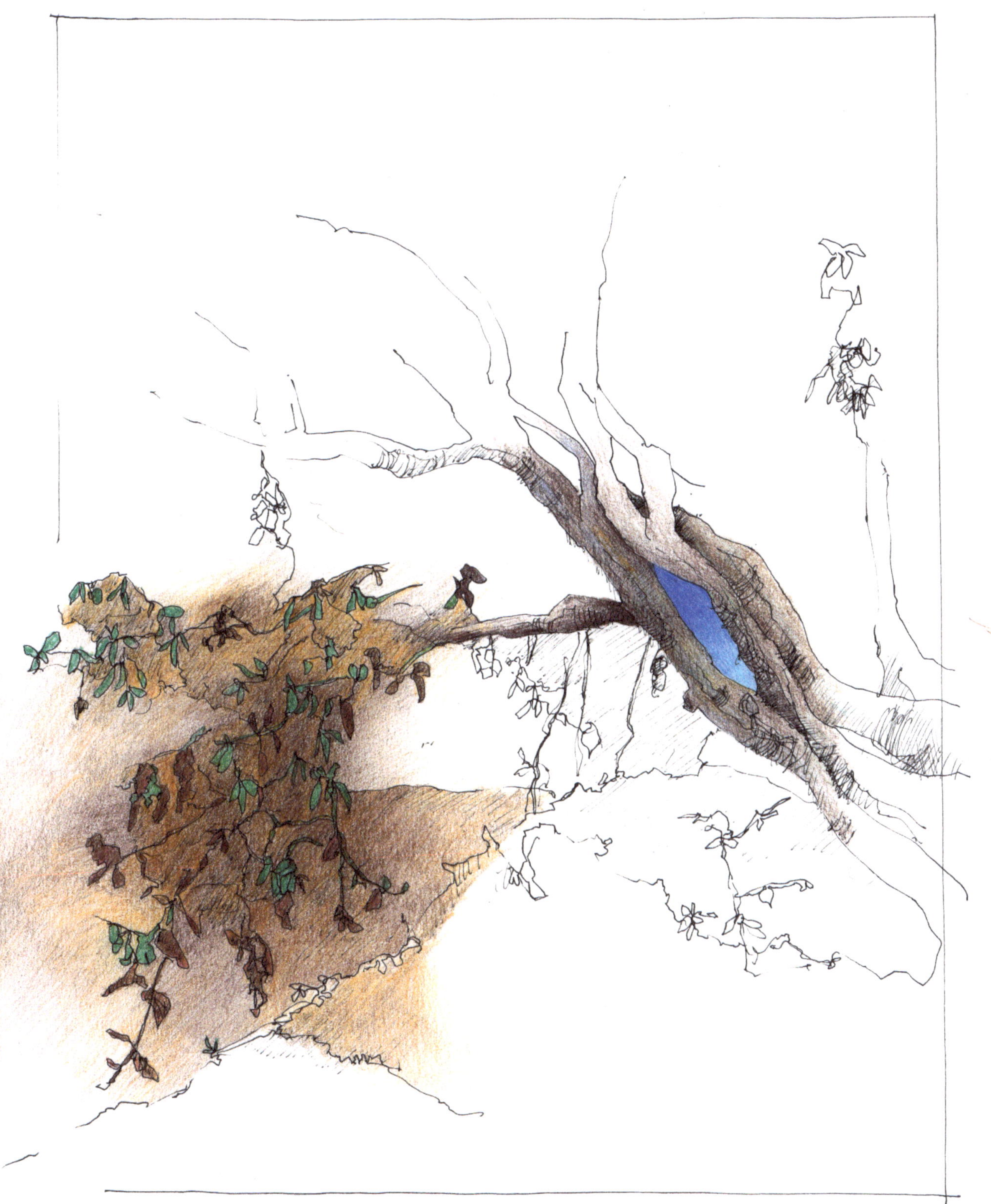

Nineteenth Summer Prayer

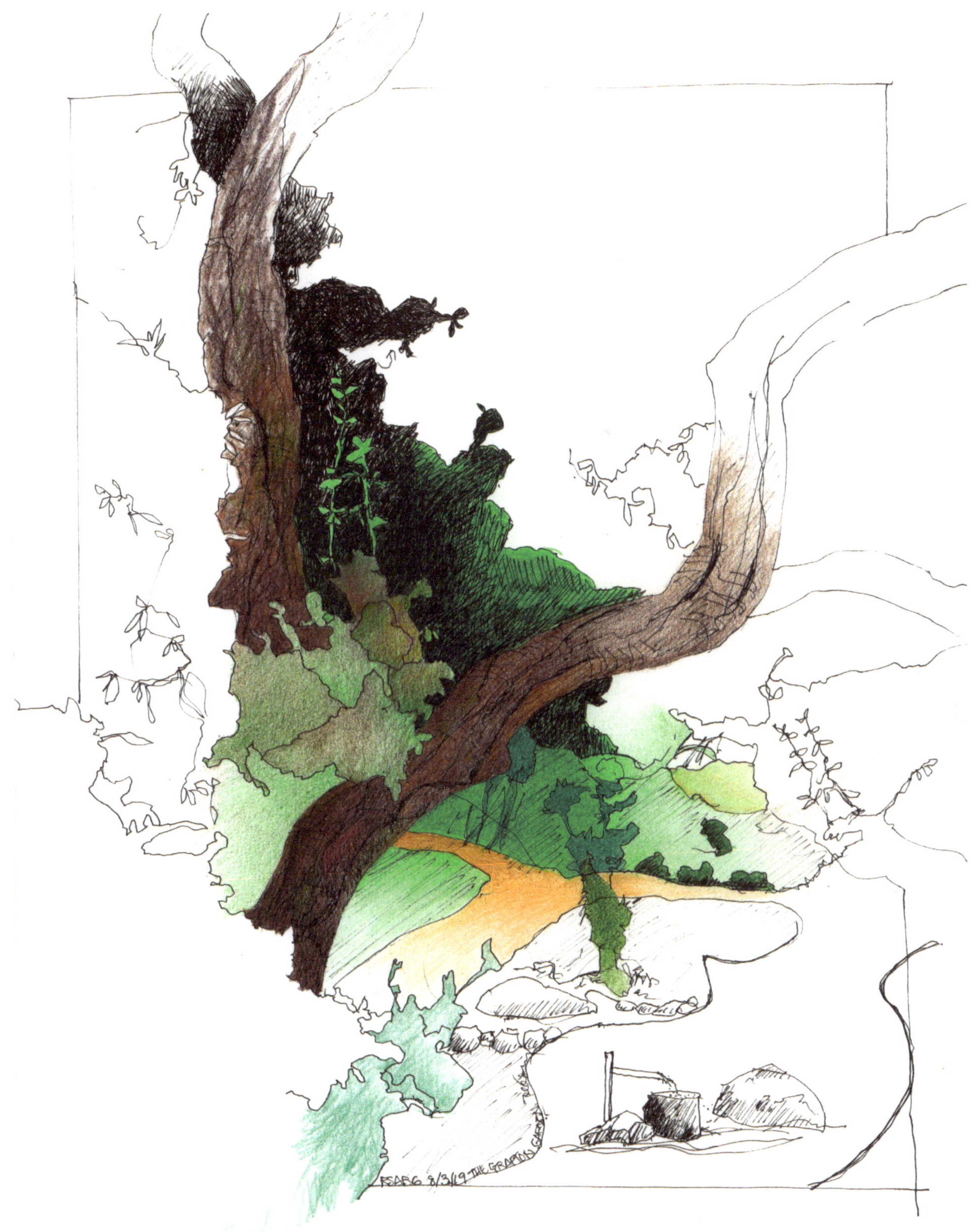

RSABG 8/3/19 THE GRAFTON GARDEN

Twentieth Summer Prayer

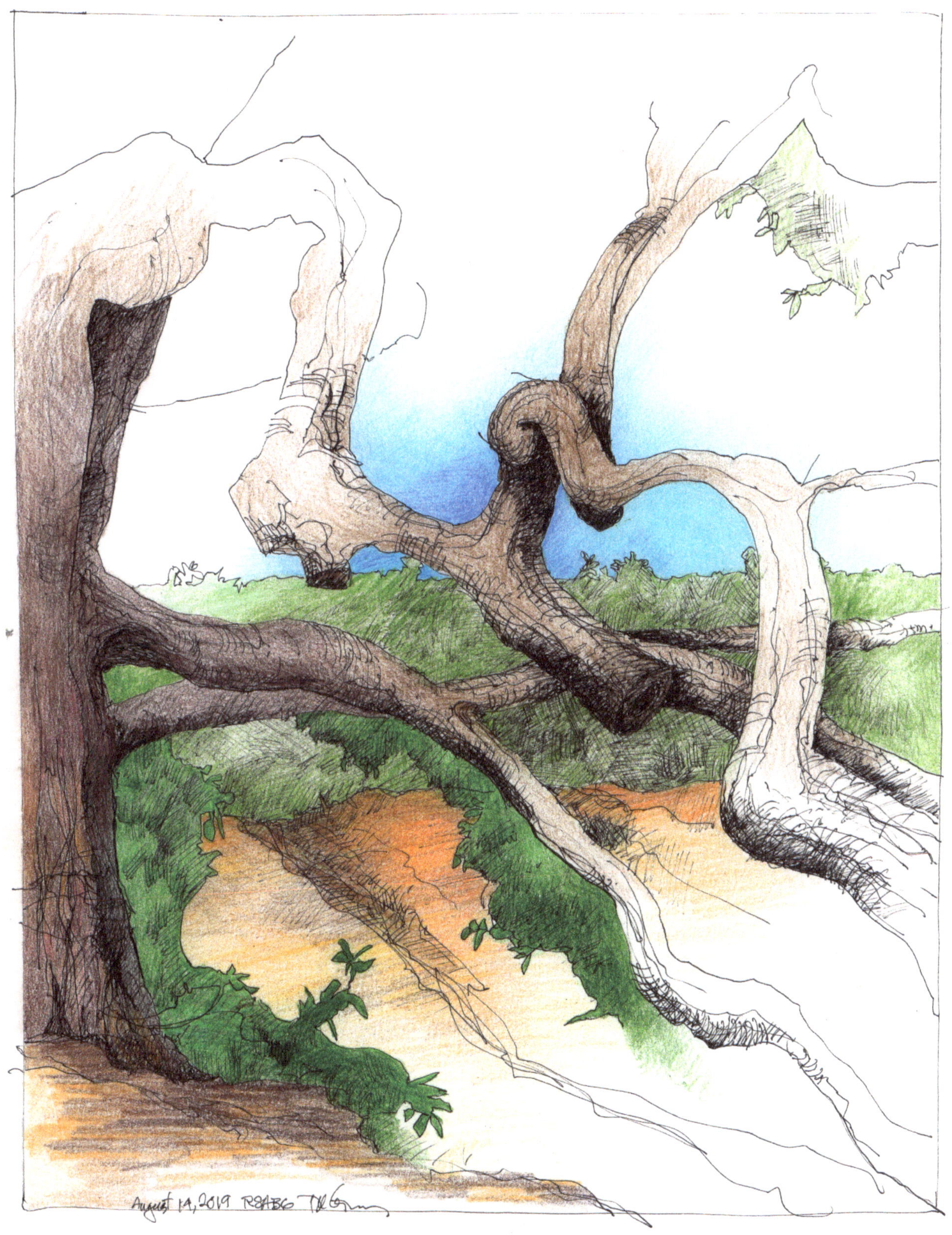

August 19, 2019 RSABG T.K.

Twenty First Summer Prayer

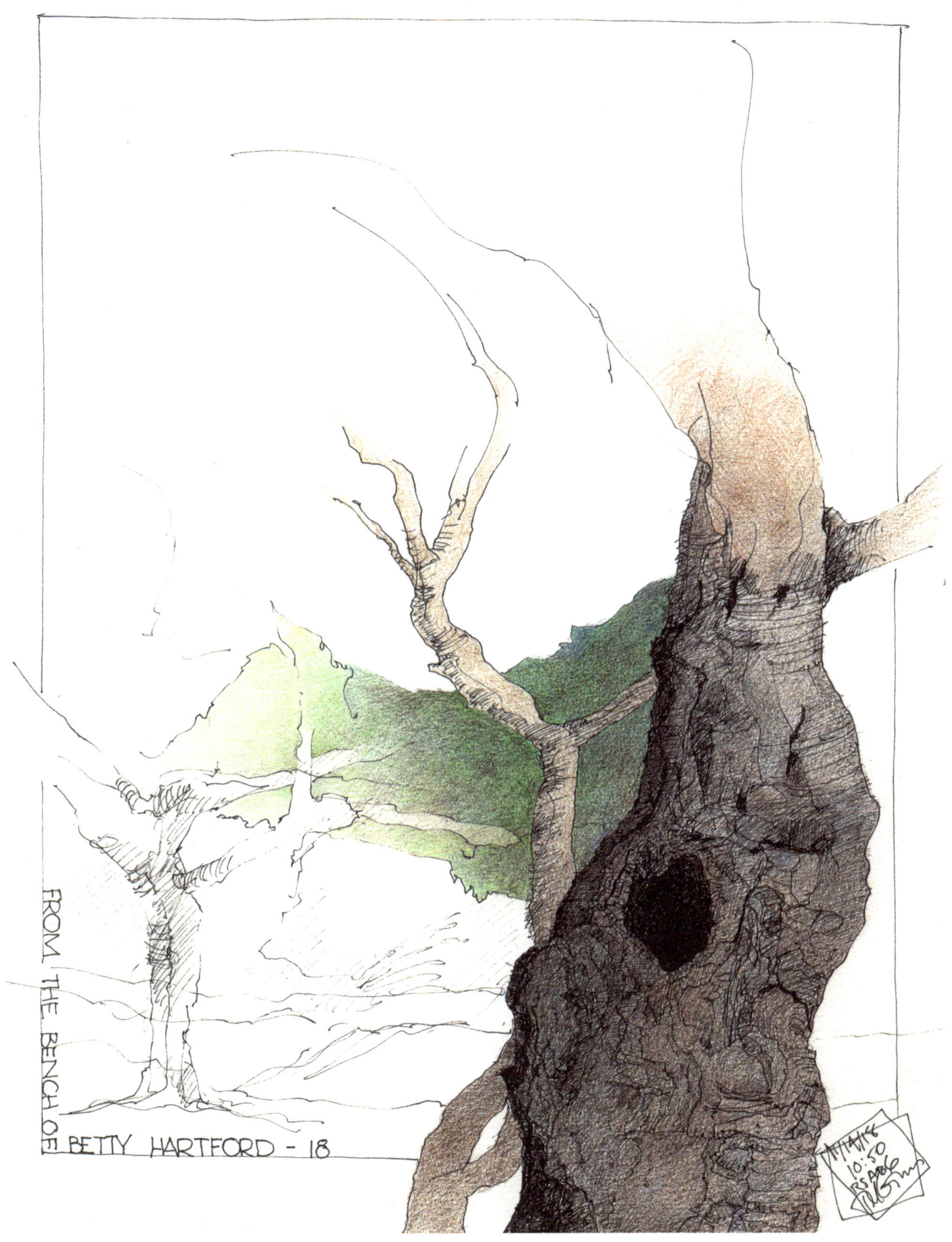

FROM THE BENCH OF
BETTY HARTFORD - 18

TERRY GIVENS

Terry Givens and his wife Carolyne were married in Claremont, California in 1961. After school and job attempts in San Diego, they returned to Claremont and he finished his education in Art History and Painting at UCR and the Claremont Graduate School.

They have lived in Claremont for the past forty-plus years. He has participated in many Claremont events, namely exhibits at the Claremont Community Foundation and as a featured artist at the Taste of Claremont, sponsored by the Rotary Club of Claremont.

Terry has exhibited in a variety of media, with sculpture at the Ankrum Gallery, the Los Angeles County Museum of Art, Chaffey College, and with drawings and paintings in a variety of galleries in Sacramento. In 2018, the Rancho Santa Ana Botanic Garden exhibited his drawings in a changing exhibition titled "Terry Givens: 100 Garden Views." He has contributed many drawings to organizations, individuals, and businesses in and around Claremont.

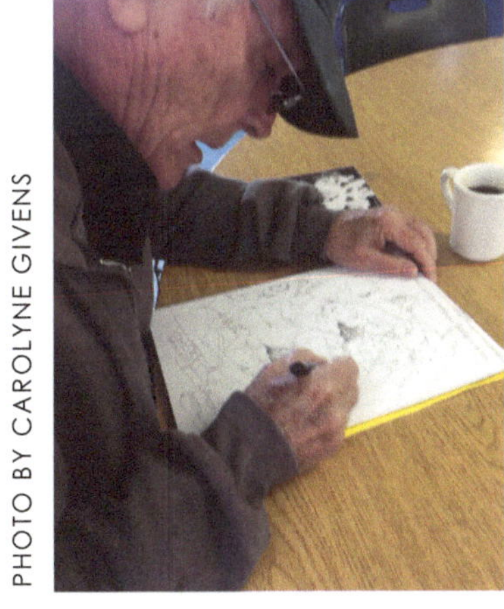

In addition, he has curated exhibitions at the Rex Wignall Gallery in Ontario and the Riverside Art Museum.

He taught art and photography in a variety of local elementary and secondary schools, as well as at local universities and colleges.

Terry and Carolyne have three grown, admirable children, four superlative grandchildren and live in Upland.

Acknowledgments

Once again I must tell you how much I appreciate Lucinda McDade (CEO) and all of the staff at the Rancho Santa Ana Botanic Garden. The Garden is always beautiful to see, walk through, stay for a while, and experience... even when I don't draw something.

I wish Shirley Neilsen Blum was still here and I could talk to her again. She was my professor in Art History at UCR during the mid-sixties and she talked us through much of the activities, strategies, and ideas of the art world. During that time, I began to understand some of the language and metaphors she used..... all of which are my reality now.

Of course, once again I must acknowledge with grace and wonder for my publisher and son Mark Givens for his encouragement, insight, and wisdom.